Season Songs

TED HUGHES

FABER AND FABER

London · Boston

First published in 1976
by Faber and Faber Limited
3 Queen Square London WC1
Reprinted 1979
Printed in Great Britain by
Ebenezer Baylis and Son, Limited
The Trinity Press, Worcester, and London

ISBN 0 571 10890 3

Season Songs

To Carol

Contents

❄

Winter:

Spring

A March Calf

Right from the start he is dressed in his best—his blacks and his whites.
Little Fauntleroy—quiffed and glossy,
A Sunday suit, a wedding natty get-up,
Standing in dunged straw

Under cobwebby beams, near the mud wall,
Half of him legs,
Shining-eyed, requiring nothing more
But that mother's milk come back often.

Everything else is in order, just as it is.
Let the summer skies hold off, for the moment.
This is just as he wants it.
A little at a time, of each new thing, is best.

Too much and too sudden is too frightening—
When I block the light, a bulk from space,
To let him in to his mother for a suck,
He bolts a yard or two, then freezes,

Staring from every hair in all directions,
Ready for the worst, shut up in his hopeful religion,
A little syllogism
With a wet blue-reddish muzzle, for God's thumb.

You see all his hopes bustling
As he reaches between the worn rails towards
The topheavy oven of his mother.
He trembles to grow, stretching his curl-tip tongue—

What did cattle ever find here
To make this dear little fellow
So eager to prepare himself?
He is already in the race, and quivering to win—

His new purpled eyeball swivel-jerks
In the elbowing push of his plans.
Hungry people are getting hungrier,
Butchers developing expertise and markets,

But he just wobbles his tail—and glistens
Within his dapper profile
Unaware of how his whole lineage
Has been tied up.

He shivers for feel of the world licking his side.
He is like an ember—one glow
Of lighting himself up
With the fuel of himself, breathing and brightening.

Soon he'll plunge out, to scatter his seething joy,
To be present at the grass,
To be free on the surface of such a wideness,
To find himself himself. To stand. To moo.

The River in March

Now the river is rich, but her voice is low.
It is her Mighty Majesty the sea
Travelling among the villages incognito.

Now the river is poor. No song, just a thin mad whisper.
The winter floods have ruined her.
She squats between draggled banks, fingering her rags and rubbish.

And now the river is rich. A deep choir.
It is the lofty clouds, that work in heaven,
Going on their holiday to the sea.

The river is poor again. All her bones are showing.
Through a dry wig of bleached flotsam she peers up ashamed
From her slum of sticks.

Now the river is rich, collecting shawls and minerals.
Rain brought fatness, but she takes ninety-nine percent
Leaving the fields just one percent to survive on.

And now she is poor. Now she is East wind sick.
She huddles in holes and corners. The brassy sun gives her a headache.
She has lost all her fish. And she shivers.

But now once more she is rich. She is viewing her lands.
A hoard of king-cups spills from her folds, it blazes, it cannot be hidden.
A salmon, a sow of solid silver,

Bulges to glimpse it.

March Morning Unlike Others

Blue haze. Bees hanging in air at the hive-mouth.
Crawling in prone stupor of sun
On the hive-lip. Snowdrops. Two buzzards,
Still-wings, each
Magnetised to the other
Float orbits.
Cattle standing warm. Lit, happy stillness.
A raven, under the hill,
Coughing among bare oaks.
Aircraft, elated, splitting blue.
Leisure to stand. The knee-deep mud at the trough
Stiffening. Lambs freed to be foolish.

The earth invalid, dropsied, bruised, wheeled
Out into the sun,
After the frightful operation.
She lies back, wounds undressed to the sun,
To be healed,
Sheltered from the sneapy chill creeping North wind,
Leans back, eyes closed, exhausted, smiling
Into the sun. Perhaps dozing a little.
While we sit, and smile, and wait, and know
She is not going to die.

Spring Nature Notes

1

The sun lies mild and still on the yard stones.

The clue is a solitary daffodil—the first.

And the whole air struggling in soft excitements
Like a woman hurrying into her silks.
Birds everywhere zipping and unzipping
Changing their minds, in soft excitements,
Warming their wings and trying their voices.

The trees still spindle bare.

Beyond them, from the warmed blue hills
An exhilaration swirls upward, like a huge fish.

As under a waterfall, in the bustling pool.

Over the whole land
Spring thunders down in brilliant silence.

2

An oak tree on the first day of April
Is as bare as the same oak in December
But it looks completely different.

Now it bristles, it is a giant brazier
Of invisible glare, an invisible sun.
The oak tree's soul has returned and flames its strength.
You feel those rays—even though you can't see them
They touch you.

(Just as you feel touched, and turn round
To meet eyes staring straight at the back of your head.)

3

A spurt of daffodils, stiff, quivering—
Plumes, blades, creases, Guardsmen
At attention

Like sentinels at the tomb of a great queen.
(Not like what they are—the advance guard
Of a drunken slovenly army

Which will leave this whole place wrecked.)

4

The crocuses are too naked. Space shakes them.
They remind you the North Sky is one vast hole
With black space blowing out of it
And that you too are being worn thin
By the blowing atoms of decomposed stars.

Down the moonbeams come hares
Hobbling on their square wheels.
What space has left, the hares eat.

What the hares do not want
Looks next morning like the leavings of picnickers
Who were kidnapped by a fright from space.

The crocus bulb stays hidden—veteran
Of terrors beyond man.

5

Spring bulges the hills.
The bare trees creak and shift.
Some buds have burst in tatters—
Like firework stubs.

But winter's lean bullocks
Only pretend to eat
The grass that will not come.

Then they bound like lambs, they twist in the air
They bounce their half tons of elastic
When the bale of hay breaks open.

They gambol from heap to heap,
Finally stand happy chewing their beards
Of last summer's dusty whiskers.

6

With arms swinging, a tremendous skater
On the flimsy ice of space,
The earth leans into its curve—

Thrilled to the core, some flies have waded out
An inch onto my window, to stand on the sky
And try their buzz.

April Birthday

When your birthday brings the world under your window
   And the song-thrush sings wet-throated in the dew
And aconite and primrose are unsticking the wrappers
   Of the package that has come today for you

           Lambs bounce out and stand astonished
           Puss willow pushes among bare branches
           Sooty hawthorns shiver into emerald

                    And a new air
           Nuzzles the sugary
           Buds of the chestnut. A groundswell and a stir
           Billows the silvered
           Violet silks
           Of the south—a tenderness
           Lifting through all the
           Gently-breasted
           Counties of England.

When the swallow snips the string that holds the world in
   And the ring-dove claps and nearly loops the loop
You just can't count everything that follows in a tumble
   Like a whole circus tumbling through a hoop

           Grass in a mesh of all flowers floundering
           Sizzling leaves and blossoms bombing
           Nestlings hissing and groggy-legged insects

                    And the trees
           Stagger, they stronger
           Brace their boles and biceps under
           The load of gift. And the hills float
           Light as bubble glass
           On the smoke-blue evening

And rabbits are bobbing everywhere, and a thrush
Rings coolly in a far corner. A shiver of green
Strokes the darkening slope as the land
Begins her labour.

Icecrust and Snowflake

A polished glancing. A blue frost-bright dawn.

And the ox's hoof-quag mire
At the ice-cumbered trough has so far protected
A primrose.

And the wild mares, in the moor hollow,
Stand stupid with bliss
Among the first miraculous foal-flowers.

They are weeping for joy in a wind

That blows through the flint of the ox's horn.

2

The North Wind brought you too late

To the iron bar, rusted sodden
In the red soil.

The salmon weightless
In the flag of depth
Green as engine oil.

A snowflake in April
That touched, that registered
Was felt.

Solitary signal
Of a storm too late to get in

Past the iron bar's leaf

Through the window
Of the salmon's egg
With its eager eye.

Deceptions

The oak is a railway station.
Wait there for the spring.
Will it stop for you?
The famous express blurs through—
Where is it going?
Leaving all the oak's fronds in a blush and agitation—

          Nor will you catch it at the ash.

The March hare brings the spring
For you personally.
He is too drunk to deliver it.
He loses it on some hare-brained folly—
Now you will never recover it.
All year he will be fleeing and flattening his ears and fleeing—

          Eluding your fury.

With the cherry bloom for her fancy dress
Spring is giving a party—
And we have been invited.
We've just arrived, all excited,
When she rushes out past us weeping, tattered and dirty—
Wind and rain are wrecking the place

          And we can only go home.

Spring will marry you. A promise!
Cuckoo brings the message: May.
O new clothes! O get your house ready!
Expectation keeps you starry.
But at which church and on what day?
All month you sit waiting, and in June you know that it's off.

          And the cuckoo has started to laugh.

Summer

Swifts

Fifteenth of May. Cherry blossom. The swifts
Materialise at the tip of a long scream
Of needle. "Look! They're back! Look!" And they're gone
On a steep

Controlled scream of skid
Round the house-end and away under the cherries. Gone.
Suddenly flickering in sky summit, three or four together,
Gnat-whisp frail, and hover-searching, and listening

For air-chills—are they too early? With a bowing
Power-thrust to left, then to right, then a flicker they
Tilt into a slide, a tremble for balance,
Then a lashing down disappearance

Behind elms.
                        They've made it again,
Which means the globe's still working, the Creation's
Still waking refreshed, our summer's
Still all to come—
                        And here they are, here they are again
Erupting across yard stones
Shrapnel-scatter terror. Frog-gapers,
Speedway goggles, international mobsters—

A bolas of three or four wire screams
Jockeying across each other
On their switchback wheel of death.
They swat past, hard-fletched,

Veer on the hard air, toss up over the roof,
And are gone again. Their mole-dark labouring,
Their lunatic limber scramming frenzy
And their whirling blades

Sparkle out into blue—

                          Not ours any more.

Rats ransacked their nests so now they shun us.
Round luckier houses now
They crowd their evening dirt-track meetings,

Racing their discords, screaming as if speed-burned,
Head-height, clipping the doorway
With their leaden velocity and their butterfly lightness,
Their too much power, their arrow-thwack into the eaves.

Every year a first-fling, nearly-flying
Misfit flopped in our yard,
Groggily somersaulting to get airborne.
He bat-crawled on his tiny useless feet, tangling his flails

Like a broken toy, and shrieking thinly
Till I tossed him up—then suddenly he flowed away under
His bowed shoulders of enormous swimming power,
Slid away along levels wobbling

On the fine wire they have reduced life to,
And crashed among the raspberries.
Then followed fiery hospital hours
In a kitchen. The moustached goblin savage

Nested in a scarf. The bright blank
Blind, like an angel, to my meat-crumbs and flies.
Then eyelids resting. Wasted clingers curled.
The inevitable balsa death.

                          Finally burial

For the husk
Of my little Apollo—

The charred scream
Folded in its huge power.

Mackerel Song

While others sing the mackerel's armour
His stub scissor head and his big blurred eye
And the flimsy savagery of his onset
I sing his simple hunger.

While others sing the mackerel's swagger
His miniature ocelot oil-green stripings
And his torpedo solidity of thump
I sing his gormless plenty.

While others sing the mackerel's fury
The belly-tug lightning-trickle of his evasions
And the wrist-thick muscle of his last word
I sing his loyal come-back.

While others sing the mackerel's acquaintance
The soap of phosphorus he lathers on your fingers
The midget gut and the tropical racer's torso
I sing his scorched sweetness.

While others sing the mackerel's demise
His ultimatum to be cooked instantly
And the shock of his decay announcement
I sing how he makes the rich summer seas

A million times richer

With the gift of his millions.

Hay

The grass is happy
To run like a sea, to be glossed like a mink's fur
By polishing wind.
Her heart is the weather.
She loves nobody
        Least of all the farmer who leans on the gate.

The grass is happy
When the June sun roasts the foxgloves in the hedges.
She comes into her flower.
She lifts her skirts.
It does not concern her
        The pondering farmer has begun to hope.

The grass is happy
To open her scents, like a dress, through the county,
Drugging light hearts
To heavy betrothals
And next April's Fools,
        While pensioners puzzle where life went so airily.

The grass is happy
When the spinner tumbles her, she silvers and she sweetens.
Plain as a castle
The hare looks for home
And the dusty farmer
        For a hand-shaped cloud and a yellow evening.

Happy the grass
To be wooed by the farmer, who wins her and brings her to church in
                      her beauty,
Bride of the Island.
Luckless the long-drawn
Aeons of Eden
        Before he came to mow.

Sheep

The sheep has stopped crying.
All morning in her wire-mesh compound
On the lawn, she has been crying
For her vanished lamb. Yesterday they came.
Then her lamb could stand, in a fashion,
And make some tiptoe cringing steps.
Now he has disappeared.
He was only half the proper size,
And his cry was wrong. It was not
A dry little hard bleat, a baby-cry
Over a flat tongue, it was human,
It was a despairing human smooth Oh!
Like no lamb I ever heard. Its hindlegs
Cowered in under its lumped spine,
Its feeble hips leaned towards
Its shoulders for support. Its stubby
White wool pyramid head, on a tottery neck,
Had sad and defeated eyes, pinched, pathetic,
Too small, and it cried all the time
Oh! Oh! staggering towards
Its alert, baffled, stamping, storming mother
Who feared our intentions. He was too weak
To find her teats, or to nuzzle up in under,
He hadn't the gumption. He was fully
Occupied just standing, then shuffling
Towards where she'd removed to. She knew
He wasn't right, she couldn't
Make him out. Then his rough-curl legs,
So stoutly built, and hooved
With real quality tips,
Just got in the way, like a loose bundle
Of firewood he was cursed to manage,
Too heavy for him, lending sometimes

Some support, but no strength, no real help.
When we sat his mother on her tail, he mouthed her teat,
Slobbered a little, but after a minute
Lost aim and interest, his muzzle wandered,
He was managing a difficulty
Much more urgent and important. By evening
He could not stand. It was not
That he could not thrive, he was born
With everything but the will—
That can be deformed, just like a limb.
Death was more interesting to him.
Life could not get his attention.
So he died, with the yellow birth-mucus
Still in his cardigan.
He did not survive a warm summer night.
Now his mother has started crying again.
The wind is oceanic in the elms
And the blossom is all set.

2

What is it this time the dark barn again
Where men jerk me off my feet
And shout over me with murder voices
And do something painful to somewhere on my body

Why am I grabbed by the leg and dragged from my friends
Where I was hidden safe though it was hot
Why am I dragged into the light and whirled onto my back
Why am I sat up on my rear end with my legs splayed

A man grips me helpless his knees grip me helpless
What is that buzzer what is it coming
Buzzing like a big fierce insect on a long tangling of snake
What is the man doing to me with his buzzing thing

That I cannot see he is pressing it into me
I surrender I let my legs kick I let myself be killed

I let him hoist me about he twists me flat
In a leverage of arms and legs my neck pinned under his ankle

While he does something dreadful down the whole length of my belly
My little teats stand helpless and terrified as he buzzes around them

Poor old ewe! She peers around from her ridiculous position.
Cool intelligent eyes, of grey-banded agate and amber,

Eyes deep and clear with feeling and understanding
While her monster hooves dangle helpless
And a groan like no bleat vibrates in her squashed windpipe
And the cutter buzzes at her groin and her fleece piles away

Now it buzzes at her throat and she emerges whitely
More and more grotesquely female and nude
Paunchy and skinny, while her old rug, with its foul tassels
Heaps from her as a foam-stiff, foam-soft, yoke-yellow robe

Numbed all over she suddenly feels much lighter
She feels herself free, her legs are her own and she scrambles up
Waiting for that grapple of hands to fling her down again
She stands in the opened arch of his knees she is facing a bright
                                                                    doorway

With a real bleat to comfort the lamb in herself
She trots across the threshold and makes one high clearing bound
To break from the cramp of her fright
And surprised by her new lightness and delighted

She trots away, noble-nosed, her pride unsmirched.
Her greasy winter-weight stays coiled on the foul floor, for
                                    somebody else to bother about.
She has a beautiful wet green brand on her bobbing brand-new
                                                                    backside,
She baas, she has come off best.

33

3

The mothers have come back
From the shearing, and behind the hedge
The woe of sheep is like a battlefield
In the evening, when the fighting is over,
And the cold begins, and the dew falls,
And bowed women move with water.
Mother mother mother the lambs
Are crying, and the mothers are crying.
Nothing can resist that probe, that cry
Of a lamb for its mother, or an ewe's crying
For its lamb. The lambs cannot find
Their mothers among those shorn strangers.
A half-hour they have lamented,
Shaking their voices in desperation.
Bald brutal-voiced mothers braying out,
Flat-tongued lambs chopping off hopelessness.
Their hearts are in panic, their bodies
Are a mess of woe, woe they cry,
They mingle their trouble, a music
Of worse and worse distress, a worse entangling,
They hurry out little notes
With all their strength, cries searching this way and that.
The mothers force out sudden despair, blaaa!
On restless feet, with wild heads.

Their anguish goes on and on, in the June heat.
Only slowly their hurt dies, cry by cry,
As they fit themselves to what has happened.

Apple Dumps

After the fiesta, the beauty-contests, the drunken wrestling
Of the blossom
Come some small ugly swellings, the dwarfish truths
Of the prizes.

After blushing and confetti, the breeze-blown bridesmaids, the
                                                    shadowed snapshots
Of the trees in bloom
Come the gruelling knuckles, and the cracked housemaid's hands,
The workworn morning plainness of apples.

Unearthly was the hope, the wet star melting the gland,
Staggering the offer—
But pawky the real returns, not easy to see,
Dull and leaf-green, hidden, still-bitter, and hard.

The orchard flared wings, like a new heaven, a dawn-lipped
                                                    apocalypse
Kissing the sleeper—
The apples emerge, in the sun's black shade, among stricken trees,
A straggle of survivors, nearly all ailing.

Work and Play

The swallow of summer, she toils all summer,
A blue-dark knot of glittering voltage,
A whiplash swimmer, a fish of the air.
 But the serpent of cars that crawls through the dust
 In shimmering exhaust
 Searching to slake
 Its fever in ocean
 Will play and be idle or else it will bust.

The swallow of summer, the barbed harpoon,
She flings from the furnace, a rainbow of purples,
Dips her glow in the pond and is perfect.
 But the serpent of cars that collapsed at the beach
 Disgorges its organs
 A scamper of colours
 Which roll like tomatoes
 Nude as tomatoes
 With sand in their creases
 To cringe in the sparkle of rollers and screech.

The swallow of summer, the seamstress of summer,
She scissors the blue into shapes and she sews it,
She draws a long thread and she knots it at corners.
 But the holiday people
 Are laid out like wounded
 Flat as in ovens
 Roasting and basting
 With faces of torment as space burns them blue
 Their heads are transistors
 Their teeth grit on sand grains
 Their lost kids are squalling
 While man-eating flies
 Jab electric shock needles but what can they do?

They can climb in their cars with raw bodies, raw faces
    And start up the serpent
    And headache it homeward
    A car full of squabbles
    And sobbing and stickiness
    With sand in their crannies
    Inhaling petroleum
    That pours from the foxgloves
    While the evening swallow
The swallow of summer, cartwheeling through crimson,
Touches the honey-slow river and turning
Returns to the hand stretched from under the eaves—
A boomerang of rejoicing shadow.

The Harvest Moon

The flame-red moon, the harvest moon,
Rolls along the hills, gently bouncing,
A vast balloon,
Till it takes off, and sinks upward
To lie in the bottom of the sky, like a gold doubloon.

The harvest moon has come,
Booming softly through heaven, like a bassoon.
And earth replies all night, like a deep drum.

So people can't sleep,
So they go out where elms and oak trees keep
A kneeling vigil, in a religious hush.
The harvest moon has come!

And all the moonlit cows and all the sheep
Stare up at her petrified, while she swells
Filling heaven, as if red hot, and sailing
Closer and closer like the end of the world

Till the gold fields of stiff wheat
Cry "We are ripe, reap us!" and the rivers
Sweat from the melting hills.

The Golden Boy

In March he was buried
            And nobody cried
Buried in the dirt
            Nobody protested
Where grubs and insects
            That nobody knows
With outer-space faces
            That nobody loves
Can make him their feast
            As if nobody cared.

But the Lord's mother
            Full of her love
Found him underground
            And wrapped him with love
As if he were her baby
            Her own born love
She nursed him with miracles
            And starry love
And he began to live
            And to thrive on her love

He grew night and day
            And his murderers were glad
He grew like a fire
            And his murderers were happy
He grew lithe and tall
            And his murderers were joyful
He toiled in the fields
            And his murderers cared for him
He grew a gold beard
            And his murderers laughed.

39

With terrible steel
		They slew him in the furrow
With terrible steel
		They beat his bones from him
With terrible steel
		They ground him to powder
They baked him in ovens
		They sliced him on tables
They ate him they ate him
		They ate him they ate him

Thanking the Lord
Thanking the Wheat
Thanking the Bread
For bringing them Life
Today and Tomorrow
Out of the dirt.

Autumn

Leaves

Who's killed the leaves?
Me, says the apple, I've killed them all.
Fat as a bomb or a cannonball
I've killed the leaves.

Who sees them drop?
Me, says the pear, they will leave me all bare
So all the people can point and stare.
I see them drop.

Who'll catch their blood?
Me, me, me, says the marrow, the marrow.
I'll get so rotund that they'll need a wheelbarrow.
I'll catch their blood.

Who'll make their shroud?
Me, says the swallow, there's just time enough
Before I must pack all my spools and be off.
I'll make their shroud.

Who'll dig their grave?
Me, says the river, with the power of the clouds
A brown deep grave I'll dig under my floods.
I'll dig their grave.

Who'll be their parson?
Me, says the Crow, for it is well-known
I study the bible right down to the bone.
I'll be their parson.

Who'll be chief mourner?
Me, says the wind, I will cry through the grass
The people will pale and go cold when I pass.
I'll be chief mourner.

Who'll carry the coffin?
Me, says the sunset, the whole world will weep
To see me lower it into the deep.
I'll carry the coffin.

Who'll sing a psalm?
Me, says the tractor, with my gear grinding glottle
I'll plough up the stubble and sing through my throttle.
I'll sing the psalm.

Who'll toll the bell?
Me, says the robin, my song in October
Will tell the still gardens the leaves are over.
I'll toll the bell.

Autumn Nature Notes

1

The Laburnum top is silent, quite still
In the afternoon yellow September sunlight,
A few leaves yellowing, all its seeds fallen.

Till the goldfinch comes, with a twitching chirrup,
A suddenness, a startlement, at a branch-end.
Then sleek as a lizard, and alert, and abrupt
She enters the thickness, and a machine starts up
Of chitterings, and a tremor of wings, and trillings—
The whole tree trembles and thrills.
It is the engine of her family.
She stokes it full, then flirts out to a branch-end
Showing her barred face identity mask

Then with eerie delicate whistle-chirrup whisperings
She launches away, towards the infinite

And the laburnum subsides to empty.

2

The sun finally tolerable.
The sunflowers tired out, like old gardeners.
Cabbage-white butterflies eddying
In the still pool of what is left to them.
The buddleia's last cones of lilac intoxicant
Crusted with Peacock butterflies and Red Admirals.

A raven, orbiting elm-high, lazily,
Two cronks to each circuit.
Sky sprinkled with forked martins
Swallows glittering their voices.

Now a cooler push, rocking the mesh of soft-edged shadows.

So we sit on the earth which is warmed
And sweetened and ripened
By the furnace
On which the door has just about closed.

3

The chestnut splits its padded cell.
It opens an African eye.

A cabinet-maker, an old master
In the root of things, has done it again.

Its slippery gloss is a swoon,
A peek over the edge into—what?

Down the well-shaft of swirly grain,
Past the generous hands that lifted the May-lamps,

Into the Fairytale of a royal tree
That does not know about conkers

Or the war-games of boys.
Invisible though he is, this plump mare

Bears a tall armoured rider towards
The mirk-forest of rooty earth.

He rides to fight the North corner.
He must win a sunbeam princess

From the cloud castle of the rains.
If he fails, evil faces,

Jaws without eyes, will tear him to pieces.
If he succeeds, and has the luck

To snatch his crown from the dragon
Which resembles a slug

He will reign over our garden
For two hundred years.

4

When the Elm was full
When it heaved and all its tautnesses drummed
Like a full-sail ship

It was just how I felt.
Waist-deep, I ploughed through the lands,
I leaned at horizons, I bore down on strange harbours.

As the sea is a sail-ship's root
So the globe was mine.
When the swell lifted the crow from the Elm-top
Both Poles were my home, they rocked me and supplied me.

But now the Elm is still
All its frame bare
Its leaves are a carpet for the cabbages

And it stands engulfed in the peculiar golden light
With which Eternity's flash
Photographed the sudden cock pheasant—

Engine whinneying, the fire-ball bird clatters up,
Shuddering full-throttle
Its three tongued tail-tip writhing

And the Elm stands, astonished, wet with light,

And I stand, dazzled to my bones, blinded.

5

Through all the orchard's boughs
A honey-colour stillness, a hurrying stealth,
A quiet migration of all that can escape now.

Under ripe apples, a snapshot album is smouldering.

With a bare twig,
Glow-dazed, I coax its stubborn feathers.
A gold furred flame. A blue tremor of the air.

The fleshless faces dissolve, one by one,
As they peel open. Blackenings, shrivellings
To grey flutter. The clump's core hardens. Everything

Has to be gone through. Every corpuscle
And its gleam. Everything must go.
My heels squeeze wet mulch, and my crouch aches.

A wind-swell lifts through the oak.
Scorch-scathed, crisping, a fleeing bonfire
Hisses in invisible flames—and the flame-roar.

An alarmed blackbird, lean, alert, scolds
The everywhere slow exposure—flees, returns.

6

Water-wobbling blue-sky-puddled October.
The distance microscopic, the ditches brilliant.
Flowers so low-powered and fractional
They are not in any book.

I walk on high fields feeling the bustle
Of the million earth-folk at their fair.
Fieldfares early, exciting foreigners.
A woodpigeon pressing over, important as a policeman.

A far Bang! Then Bang! and a litter of echoes—
Country pleasures. The farmer's guest,
In U.S. combat green, will be trampling brambles,
Waving his gun like a paddle.

I thought I'd brushed with a neighbour—
Fox-reek, a warm web, rich as creosote,
Draping the last watery blackberries—
But it was the funeral service.

Two nights he has lain, patient in his position,
Puckered under the first dews of being earth,
Crumpled like dead bracken. His reek will cling
To his remains till spring.

Then I shall steal his fangs, and wear them, and honour them.

7

Three pale foxglove lamp-mantles, in full flare
Among gritty burned-out spires of old foxgloves
Under needling sleet, in a crossing squall.

This last week, a baby hand of blossom
Among corroded leaves, over windfall apples.

Every apple a festival of small slugs

Probably thinking their good time had just started.

So the old year, tired,
Smiles over his tools, fondling them a little,
As he puts them away.

8

Oceanic windy dawn.
Shapes grab at the window.
Ravens go head over heels.
The flood has scoured the sky.

No going on deck today.
I see, through the submerged window,
That the quince tree, which yesterday
Still clung to a black leaf, has lost it.

The Seven Sorrows

The first sorrow of autumn
Is the slow goodbye
Of the garden who stands so long in the evening—
A brown poppy head,
The stalk of a lily,
And still cannot go.

The second sorrow
Is the empty feet
Of the pheasant who hangs from a hook with his brothers.
The woodland of gold
Is folded in feathers
With its head in a bag.

And the third sorrow
Is the slow goodbye
Of the sun who has gathered the birds and who gathers
The minutes of evening,
The golden and holy
Ground of the picture.

The fourth sorrow
Is the pond gone black
Ruined and sunken the city of water—
The beetle's palace,
The catacombs
Of the dragonfly.

And the fifth sorrow
Is the slow goodbye
Of the woodland that quietly breaks up its camp.
One day it's gone.
It has left only litter—
Firewood, tentpoles.

And the sixth sorrow
Is the fox's sorrow
The joy of the huntsman, the joy of the hounds,
The hooves that pound
Till earth closes her ear
To the fox's prayer.

And the seventh sorrow
Is the slow goodbye
Of the face with its wrinkles that looks through the window
As the year packs up
Like a tatty fairground
That came for the children.

A Cranefly in September

She is struggling through grass-mesh—not flying,
Her wide-winged, stiff, weightless basket-work of limbs
Rocking, like an antique wain, a top-heavy ceremonial cart
Across mountain summits
(Not planing over water, dipping her tail)
But blundering with long strides, long reachings, reelings
And ginger-glistening wings
From collision to collision.
Aimless in no particular direction,
Just exerting her last to escape out of the overwhelming
Of whatever it is, legs, grass,
The garden, the county, the country, the world—

Sometimes she rests long minutes in the grass forest
Like a fairytale hero, only a marvel can help her.
She cannot fathom the mystery of this forest
In which, for instance, this giant watches—
The giant who knows she cannot be helped in any way.

Her jointed bamboo fuselage,
Her lobster shoulders, and her face
Like a pinhead dragon, with its tender moustache,
And the simple colourless church windows of her wings
Will come to an end, in mid-search, quite soon.
Everything about her, every perfected vestment
Is already superfluous.
The monstrous excess of her legs and curly feet
Are a problem beyond her.
The calculus of glucose and chitin inadequate
To plot her through the infinities of the stems.

The frayed apple leaves, the grunting raven, the defunct tractor
Sunk in nettles, wait with their multiplications
Like other galaxies.
The sky's Northward September procession, the vast soft armistice,
Like an Empire on the move,
Abandons her, tinily embattled
With her cumbering limbs and cumbered brain.

There Came a Day

There came a day that caught the summer
Wrung its neck
Plucked it
And ate it.

Now what shall I do with the trees?
The day said, the day said.
Strip them bare, strip them bare.
Let's see what is really there.

And what shall I do with the sun?
The day said, the day said.
Roll him away till he's cold and small.
He'll come back rested if he comes back at all.

And what shall I do with the birds?
The day said, the day said.
The birds I've frightened, let them flit,
I'll hang out pork for the brave tomtit.

And what shall I do with the seed?
The day said, the day said.
Bury it deep, see what it's worth.
See if it can stand the earth.

What shall I do with the people?
The day said, the day said.
Stuff them with apple and blackberry pie—
They'll love me then till the day they die.

There came this day and he was autumn.
His mouth was wide
And red as a sunset.
His tail was an icicle.

The Stag

While the rain fell on the November woodland shoulder of Exmoor
While the traffic jam along the road honked and shouted
Because the farmers were parking wherever they could
And scrambling to the bank-top to stare through the tree-fringe
Which was leafless,
The stag ran through his private forest.

While the rain drummed on the roofs of the parked cars
And the kids inside cried and daubed their chocolate and fought
And mothers and aunts and grandmothers
Were a tangle of undoing sandwiches and screwed-round gossiping
heads
Steaming up the windows,
The stag loped through his favourite valley.

While the blue horsemen down in the boggy meadow
Sodden nearly black, on sodden horses,
Spaced as at a military parade,
Moved a few paces to the right and a few to the left and felt rather
foolish
Looking at the brown impassable river,
The stag came over the last hill of Exmoor.

While everybody high-kneed it to the bank-top all along the road
Where steady men in oilskins were stationed at binoculars,
And the horsemen by the river galloped anxiously this way and that
And the cry of hounds came tumbling invisibly with their echoes down
through the draggle of trees,
Swinging across the wall of dark woodland,
The stag dropped into a strange country.

And turned at the river
Hearing the hound-pack smash the undergrowth, hearing the bell-note
Of the voice that carried all the others,

Then while his limbs all cried different directions to his lungs, which
                                             only wanted to rest,
The blue horsemen on the bank opposite
Pulled aside the camouflage of their terrible planet.

And the stag doubled back weeping and looking for home up a valley
                                             and down a valley
While the strange trees struck at him and the brambles lashed him,
And the strange earth came galloping after him carrying the
                         loll-tongued hounds to fling all over him
And his heart became just a club beating his ribs and his own hooves
                                             shouted with hounds' voices,
And the crowd on the road got back into their cars
Wet-through and disappointed.

Two Horses

1

Earth heaved, splitting. Towers
Reared out. I emerged
Behind horses, updragging with oaken twists
Swaying castles of elastic

My fortifications moved on the sky
The ploughshare my visor
Crowned by wind burn, ploughing my kingdom

Instated by the sun's sway
The fortunes of war, a famished people
Corn barons.

2

I advanced
Under the November sooty gold heaven
Among angling gulls

Behind those earth-swaying buttocks
Their roil and gleam, as in a dark wind
And the smoky foliage of their labour
Their tree-strength

Hauling earth's betrothal
From an underworld, with crocus glints
A purplish cloak-flap
The click hooves flicking
Hot circles flashing back at me lightly

Shaggy forest giants, gentle in harness
Their roots tearing and snapping
They were themselves the creaking boughs and the burden
Of earth's fleshiest ripeness, her damson tightest
Her sweetest

Earth splayed her thighs, she lay back.

3

The coulter slid effortless
The furrow's polished face, with a hiss
Coiling aside, a bow-wave that settled
Beside the poisonous brown river
As I stumbled deeper.
                            Hour after hour
The tall sweat-sleeked buttocks
Mill-wheels heavily revolving
Slackness to tautness, stretch and quiver—the vein-mapped
Watery quake-weight
In their slapping traces, drawing me deeper

Into the muffled daze and toil of their flames
Their black tails slashing sideways
The occasional purring snort

The stubble's brassy whisper
The mineral raw earth smell, the town-wind of sulphur
The knotted worms, sheared by light
The everlasting war behind the shoulder
The old ploughman still young

Furrow by furrow darkening toward summer.

4

A shout—and the dream broke, against the thorns of the headland.
Chins back, backing
Trampling sideways, a jangling of brisk metals
High-kneed, levered by cries
The plough hard over—

They had jerked awake
Into urgent seconds
Now they trod deep water, champing foam
Where were they suddenly?
                          And suddenly they knew

Like turning in a bed, and settling to sleep
The share sank

With a hard sigh, the furrow-slice sprawled over

And they bowed again to their worship.

5

The last friendly angels
Lifting their knees out of the earth, their clay-balled fetlocks
Heads down praying

And lifting me with them, into their furnace

I walked in their flames

Their long silk faces, shag-haired as old sheepdogs
Their brown eyes, like prehistoric mothers
Their mouse-belly mouths, their wire-spring whiskers
Sudden yellow teeth of the nightmare and skull

Wading the earth's wealth
In a steam of dung and sweat, to soft horse-talk

Nodding and slow in their power, climbing the sky

On the crumbling edge.

Winter

The Warrior of Winter

He met the star his enemy
   They fought the woods leafless.
He gripped his enemy.
   They trampled fields to quag.
His enemy was stronger.
   A star fought against him.

He fought his losing fight
   Up to the neck in the river.
Grimly he fought in gateways,
   He struggled among stones.
He left his strength in puddles.
   The star grew stronger.

Rising and falling
   He blundered against houses.
He gurgled for life in ditches.
   Clouds mopped his great wounds.
His shattered weapons glittered.
   The star gazed down.

Wounded and prisoner
   He slept on rotten sacking.
He gnawed bare stalks and turnip tops
   In the goose's field.
The sick sheep froze beside him.
   The star was his guard.

With bones like frozen plumbing
   He lay in the blue morning.
His teeth locked in his head
   Like the trap-frozen fox.
But he rejoiced a tear in the sun.
   Like buds his dressings softened.

Christmas Card

You have anti-freeze in the car, yes,
  But the shivering stars wade deeper.
Your scarf's tucked in under your buttons,
  But a dry snow ticks through the stubble.
Your knee-boots gleam in the fashion,
  But the moon must stay

              And stamp and cry
              As the holly the holly
              Hots its reds

Electric blanket to comfort your bedtime
  The river no longer feels its stones.
Your windows are steamed by dumpling laughter
  The snowplough's buried on the drifted moor.
Carols shake your television
  And nothing moves on the road but the wind

              Hither and thither
              The wind and three
              Starving sheep.

Redwings from Norway rattle at the clouds
  But comfortless sneezers puddle in pubs.
The robin looks in at the kitchen window
  But all care huddles to hearths and kettles.
The sun lobs one wet snowball feebly
  Grim and blue

              The dusk of the coombe
              And the swamp woodland
              Sinks with the wren.

See old lips go purple and old brows go paler.
  The stiff crow drops in the midnight silence.
Sneezes grow coughs and coughs grow painful.
  The vixen yells in the midnight garden.
You wake with the shakes and watch your breathing
  Smoke in the moonlight—silent, silent.

> Your anklebone
> And your anklebone
> Lie big in the bed.

December River

After the brown harvest of rains, express lights
Are riding behind bare poles.

As the flood clears to cider and shrinks a little,
Leaves spinning and toiling in the underboil,
I go to find salmon.

A frost-fragility hangs.
Duck-eggshell emptiness, bare to the space-freeze.
Jupiter crucified and painful. Vapour-trails keen as incisions.

Blackly
Crusty tricorne sycamore leaves are tick-tocking down
To hit the water with a hard tiny crash.

From under the slag-smoke west
The molten river comes, bulging,
With its skin of lights.

Too late now to see much
I wade into the unfolding metals.

This vein from the sky is the sea-spirit's pathway.

Here all year salmon have been their own secret.
They were the heavy slipperiness in the green oils.

The steady name—unfathomable—
In the underbrow stare-darkness.

They leapfrogged the river's fifty-mile ladder
With love-madness for strength,
Weightlifting through all its chimneys of tonnage

And came to their never-never land—to these
Gutters the breadth of a tin bath.
And dissolved

Into holes of obviousness. Anchored in strongholds
Of a total absence. Became
The transparency of their own windows.

So, day in day out, this whole summer
I offered all I had for a touch of their wealth—
I found only endlessly empty water.

But I go now, in near-darkness,
Frost, and close to Christmas, and am admitted
To glance down and see, right at my heel,
A foot under, where backwater mills rubbish,
Like a bleached hag laid out—the hooked gape
And gargoyle lobster-claw grab

Of a dead salmon, and its white shirt-button eye.

That grimace
Of getting right through to the end and beyond it—
That helm
So marvellously engineered

Discarded, an empty stencil.
A negative, pale
In the dreggy swirlings
Of earth's already beginning mastication.

I freed it, I wanted to get it
Wedged properly mine
While the moment still held open.

As I lifted its child-heavy rubbery bulk
Marbled crimson like an old woman's fire-baked thigh

The shallows below lifted
A broad bow-wave lifted and came frowning
Straight towards me, setting the whole pool rocking,

And slid under smoothness into the trench at my feet.

Into the grave of steel
Which it could still buckle.

New Year Song

Now there comes
    The Christmas rose
        But that is eerie
                too like a ghost
        Too like a creature
                preserved under glass
        A blind white fish
                from an underground lake
        Too like last year's widow
                at a window
                        And the worst cold's to come.

Now there comes
    The tight-vest lamb
        With its wriggle eel tail
                and its wintry eye
        With its ice-age mammoth
                unconcern
        Letting the aeon
                seconds go by
        With its little peg hooves
                to dot the snow
        Following its mother
                into worse cold and worse
                        And the worst cold's to come.

Now there come
    The weak-neck snowdrops
        Bouncing like fountains
                and they stop you, they make you
        Take a deep breath
                make your heart shake you
        Such a too much of a gift
                for such a mean time

Nobody knows
                    how to accept them
All you can do
                    is gaze at them baffled
                        And the worst cold's to come.

And now there comes
    The brittle crocus
        To be nibbled by the starving hares
                    to be broken by snow
        Now comes the aconite
                    purpled by cold
        A song comes into
                    the storm-cock's fancy
        And the robin and the wren
                    they rejoice like each other
        In an hour of sunlight
                    for something important
                        Though the worst cold's to come.

Snow and Snow

Snow is sometimes a she, a soft one.
  Her kiss on your cheek, her finger on your sleeve
In early December, on a warm evening,
    And you turn to meet her, saying "It's snowing!"
        But it is not. And nobody's there.
        Empty and calm is the air.

Sometimes the snow is a he, a sly one.
  Weakly he signs the dry stone with a damp spot.
Waifish he floats and touches the pond and is not.
    Treacherous-beggarly he falters, and taps at the window.
        A little longer he clings to the grass-blade tip
        Getting his grip.

Then how she leans, how furry foxwrap she nestles
  The sky with her warm, and the earth with her softness.
How her lit crowding fairytales sink through the space-silence
  To build her palace, till it twinkles in starlight—
        Too frail for a foot
        Or a crumb of soot.

Then how his muffled armies move in all night
  And we wake and every road is blockaded
Every hill taken and every farm occupied
  And the white glare of his tents is on the ceiling.
        And all that dull blue day and on into the gloaming
        We have to watch more coming.

Then everything in the rubbish-heaped world
  Is a bridesmaid at her miracle.
Dunghills and crumbly dark old barns are bowed in the chapel of her
                          sparkle,
  The gruesome boggy cellars of the wood
        Are a wedding of lace
        Now taking place.

The Warm and the Cold

Freezing dusk is closing
  Like a slow trap of steel
On trees and roads and hills and all
  That can no longer feel.
    But the carp is in its depth
      Like a planet in its heaven.
    And the badger in its bedding
      Like a loaf in the oven.
    And the butterfly in its mummy
      Like a viol in its case.
    And the owl in its feathers
      Like a doll in its lace.

Freezing dusk has tightened
  Like a nut screwed tight
On the starry aeroplane
  Of the soaring night.
    But the trout is in its hole
      Like a chuckle in a sleeper.
    The hare strays down the highway
      Like a root going deeper.
    The snail is dry in the outhouse
      Like a seed in a sunflower.
    The owl is pale on the gatepost
      Like a clock on its tower.

Moonlight freezes the shaggy world
  Like a mammoth of ice—
The past and the future
  Are the jaws of a steel vice.
    But the cod is in the tide-rip
      Like a key in a purse.
    The deer are on the bare-blown hill
      Like smiles on a nurse.

The flies are behind the plaster
Like the lost score of a jig.
Sparrows are in the ivy-clump
Like money in a pig.

Such a frost
The flimsy moon
Has lost her wits.

A star falls.

The sweating farmers
Turn in their sleep
Like oxen on spits.

Disney
Bear in Air

By Bonnie Worth

Illustrated by the Disney Storybook Artists
Designed by the Disney Global Design Group

Dear Parent/Caregiver:

Learning to read is one of the most important things a child will ever do. And now, with a little help from that silly old bear, Pooh, learning to read is easy and fun. Using only twelve vocabulary words, Pooh's Readables are the very simplest readers you will find!

With Pooh's Readables, your emerging reader will:

- Establish a strong reading foundation— twelve words at a time.

- Build vocabulary through repetition, rhyme, rhythmic patterns, and contextual clues in illustrations.

- Develop a list of common sight words.

- Identify new words with similar sounds and letter patterns.

- Read independently.

Most important of all, your child will have fun! Silly singsong stories will have your child laughing and learning every step of the way.

Random House 🏠 New York

Copyright © 2005 Disney Enterprises Inc. Based on the "Winnie the Pooh" works, by A. A. Milne and E. H. Shepard.
All rights reserved under International and Pan-American Copyright Conventions. Published in the United States
by Random House Children's Books, a division of Random House, Inc., New York, and simultaneously in Canada
by Random House of Canada Limited, Toronto, in conjunction with Disney Enterprises, Inc.
www.randomhouse.com/kids/disney

Library of Congress Cataloging-in-Publication Data

Worth, Bonnie.
Bear in air / by Bonnie Worth.
p. cm. — (Pooh's readables)

Summary: Simple phrases describe Winnie-the-Pooh's day, from
his breakfast of honey on toast to his dreams of a giant honeycomb.

ISBN 0-7364-2279-X

[1. Honey—Fiction. 2. Teddy bears—Fiction. 3. Bees—Fiction. 4. Toys—Fiction.]
I. Title. II. Series.
PZ7.W88784Bc 2005
[E]—dc22
2004016250

MANUFACTURED IN CHINA 10 9 8 7 6 5 4 3 2 1

Bear on stair.

Bear in air!

Bear in chair.

Yum!
Bear shares.

Bees.
Bees in air.
Bear sees bees.

Bear on chair.

Bees flee.

Bear flees.

Bear sees tree.
Yum!

Bear sees bee.

Bear on chair.

Bear in air.
Bees in air.

Bees see bear.

Bees flee.

Yum!
Bee sees bear.

Bear in air!

Bear shares.

Yum!

Bear in chair.

Bear on stair.

Yum!

Here are the twelve
words you just read:

bear	shares
on	yum
stair	bees
in	sees
air	flees
chair	tree

Roland the rooster lives on the
farm with his friends, but he can't
wake up on time, and Farmer Brown
decides he will have to go...

Roland,
the Sleepy Rooster

A Bedtime Story

by Lilian Murray
illustrated by Gill Guile

Copyright © 1989 by World International Publishing Limited.
All rights reserved throughout the world.
Published in Great Britain by World International Publishing Limited,
An Egmont Company, Egmont House, P.O. Box 111, Great Ducie Street, Manchester M60 3BL.
Printed in DDR. ISBN 0 7235 1265 5
Reprinted 1990

A CIP catalogue record for this book is available from the British Library

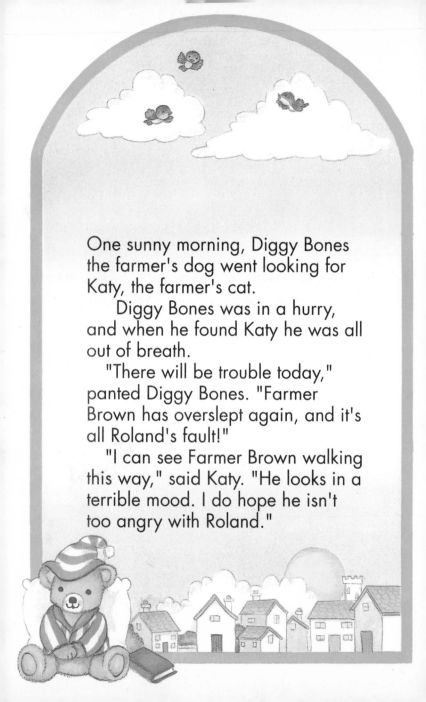

One sunny morning, Diggy Bones the farmer's dog went looking for Katy, the farmer's cat.

Diggy Bones was in a hurry, and when he found Katy he was all out of breath.

"There will be trouble today," panted Diggy Bones. "Farmer Brown has overslept again, and it's all Roland's fault!"

"I can see Farmer Brown walking this way," said Katy. "He looks in a terrible mood. I do hope he isn't too angry with Roland."

"What's the use of having a rooster if he doesn't wake us up in the morning?" demanded Farmer Brown.

"Why doesn't Roland call cock-a-doodle-doo like a good rooster should?" he said to his wife.

"He's lazy," said Farmer Brown's wife.

"I should have been milking the cows two hours ago," grumbled Farmer Brown. "Now I'll never get my work done on time today. And it's all Roland's fault."

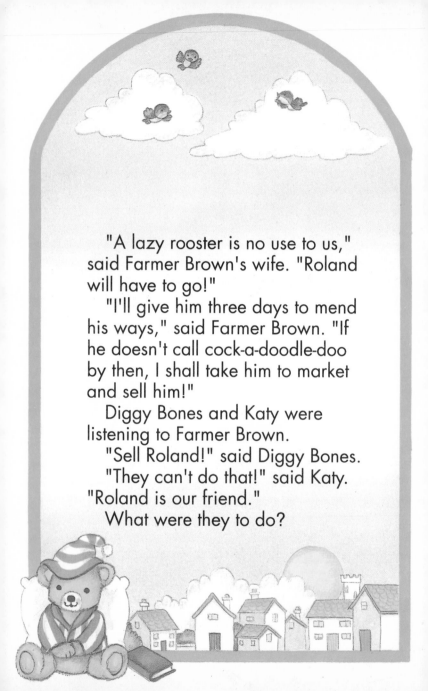

"A lazy rooster is no use to us," said Farmer Brown's wife. "Roland will have to go!"

"I'll give him three days to mend his ways," said Farmer Brown. "If he doesn't call cock-a-doodle-doo by then, I shall take him to market and sell him!"

Diggy Bones and Katy were listening to Farmer Brown.

"Sell Roland!" said Diggy Bones.

"They can't do that!" said Katy. "Roland is our friend."

What were they to do?

"We must tell Roland what Farmer Brown is going to do," said Diggy Bones. "That should make him change his lazy ways."

So the farm dog and the farm cat ran over to the barn where all the farm animals lived.

"Where is Farmer Brown?" mooed the cows. "We want to be milked."

"We want to be fed," clucked the chickens.

Diggy Bones told them what Farmer Brown had said.

"Oh, no!" clucked the chickens. "Farmer Brown can't sell Roland. What should we do without him to make us laugh. He is such a good friend."

"We all love Roland," said Diggy Bones. "But you must admit that he is a rather lazy rooster. He must wake Farmer Brown tomorrow or he really will sell him at the market."

They all looked up and saw Roland snoring happily on his perch.

"Roland!" shouted Diggy Bones.
"Come down here!"

But Roland just went on sleeping.

"I know Roland is lazy," sighed
Katy, "but he is our friend. I'll climb
up and shake him awake."

At long last Roland opened his
sleepy eyes and yawned.

"You must call cock-a-doodle-doo,
or Farmer Brown will sell you at
market," Katy told him.

Roland yawned again. "I'm sorry
I'm so lazy, but I just can't wake up
in the morning," he said.

Roland didn't want to leave the farm, so he hopped down to the other animals and asked them to help him.

"What shall I do to wake up in the morning?" he said.

"You'll have to go to bed earlier," said Katy.

"Or stay out in the cold all night like us. That will keep you awake," said the cows.

Roland listened and said he would try his best to wake up on time tomorrow.

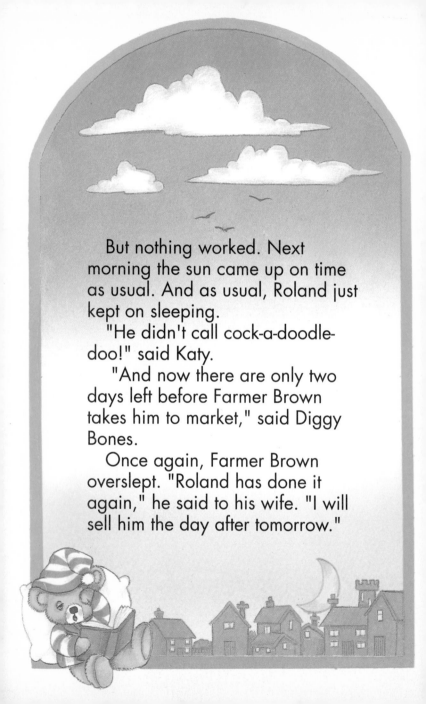

But nothing worked. Next morning the sun came up on time as usual. And as usual, Roland just kept on sleeping.

"He didn't call cock-a-doodle-doo!" said Katy.

"And now there are only two days left before Farmer Brown takes him to market," said Diggy Bones.

Once again, Farmer Brown overslept. "Roland has done it again," he said to his wife. "I will sell him the day after tomorrow."

The same thing happened again the next day.

Roland was fast asleep and didn't call cock-a-doodle-doo.

"Wake up! Wake up!" cried the animals.

Katy climbed up to Roland.

"Wake up, you lazy rooster," she said. But Roland just giggled in his sleep.

Now there was only one day left for him to call cock-a-doodle-doo before Farmer Brown took Roland off to market.

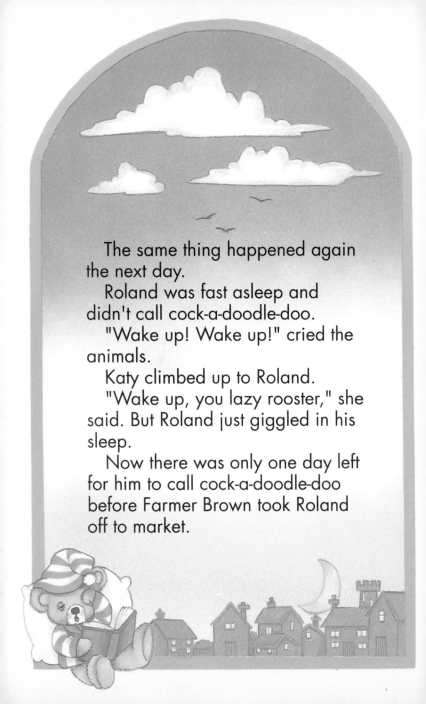

"If Roland doesn't wake up on time tomorrow, we will lose our friend," said Diggy Bones.

"And we will never see him again," said Katy.

"We don't want Roland to go," clucked the chickens.

Finally, Diggy Bones, who had been thinking very hard, said, "I've got an idea!" And he ran off into town.

When Diggy Bones came back, he was carrying a parcel. The farm animals came to see what it was.

Well, on the third morning, just as the sun came up, Roland was jolted awake by a noisy, jangling alarm clock ringing in his ear.

"Eeeeow!" screamed Roland, jumping up in the air.

"Cock-a-doodle-doo!" he called. "Cock-a-doodle-doo!"

And that's how all the farm animals got Roland, the sleepy rooster, to wake up on time again.

Every night, Diggy Bones put the alarm clock by Roland, and every morning it rang and he woke up.

So, Roland stayed on the farm and everyone was happy.

Roland called cock-a-doodle-doo on time. The cows were milked on time and the chickens were fed. And Diggy Bones the farm dog and Katy the farm cat didn't have to worry about their friend Roland any more.

Farmer Brown didn't take Roland to market after all. And he never found out about the alarm clock.

He just thought Roland had mended his ways all on his own!